The "Strategy" in Struggle

Part II of Mini-Ebook Series, Volume 2

Au'loni Media Group, LLC

Published by Au'loni Media Group, LLC, 2022.

While every precaution has been taken in the preparation of this book, the publisher assumes no responsibility for errors or omissions, or for damages resulting from the use of the information contained herein.

THE "STRATEGY" IN STRUGGLE

First edition. December 31, 2022.

ISBN: 979-8215588345

Written by Au'loni Media Group, LLC.

This book is dedicated to all the true educators, both inside the classroom and in the home. You have created the trailblazers that we have highlighted.

Personally, this series is dedicated to my first teachers who have passed on, in particular, **Mary Jones (Grandmother) and the following:**

Abraham Jones, Jr. (Eldest Uncle) Jacqueline Jones (Aunt) Nelson Jones (Uncle) Nathaniel Jones (Uncle)
Also, my loving parents and biggest inspirations: William (Spencer) Hameen and Marie Adilah Hameen

Your support, love, and dedication to enhancing my education has been and will always be invaluable.

Finally, thank you to All our amazing contributing authors: Frenchaire Gardner, Lesley Ventura, Chhavi Jain, and Tangie Holifield. This would have been impossible without your voices and passion shinging through and resonating through it.

Chapter I: Frenchaire Gardner-Do it All

"I am open to receive gratitude and joy. I deserve success and abundance. I expand in abundance, success, and love every day as I inspire those around me to do the same." Ryan Bean Insight Timer app

When I was a child I always dreamed that I would motivate large audiences on stages. I aspired to become an attorney and even majored in political science at Southern Methodist University to become one. But that is not the route that I took in life, graduating with a B average with a BA in both Psychology and Sociology. For me there was always a passion and patience for serving people. Growing up with my mama, watching her go to work day in and day out; I wanted more. My father was a not-so-successful drunk entrepreneur. He sometimes let me be the "Boss" on jobs when I was a little girl. It was so much fun calling the shots. I watched him give commands and close deals. He had time to have fun with me sometimes. He seemed to like his business.

I moved to St. Louis, Missouri from my hometown Dallas, Texas in 2011; running away from my ex-husband. I only knew two people at the time. During the first few years of living in St. Louis, I was an extrovert staying away from people. Although, that is the total opposite of my true nature. In 2014, my "sister" from college, emailed me from Rome, Italy, asking me to be her PR person and administrative assistant to get her books out to the world and make sales. Over the next 3 years, with her The English Schoolhouse books, I did just that.

Connecting with a plethora of blogs, influencers, bookstores, libraries, and media outlets for interviews, book events, features, and more. I am most proud of the appearances in Blavity.com, AfroPunk, MaterMea, Afropolitan, HereWe Read, and Kid World Citizen to name a few. The archival of a few of her children's books at the Schomburg Center for Research in Black Culture is very special to me. Quite a few of the people that I met selling The English Schoolhouse books were instrumental in making my different business ventures a success.

My business story begins with this business called Melchizedek LLC and I registered it around January 2016. I wanted to leverage my time and do something that would leave a legacy for my children Joseph Jr., Frenchaire-Two, Melchizedek, and Sarai. The goal was to produce funds while also doing something to give back to the community. I read about this opportunity in the newspaper to receive a $15,000 grant from Wells Fargo to purchase a home. At that time, I was protecting families with insurance at a large insurance company.

I knew nothing about real estate other than I wanted a house and a house was on my vision board. After a full day of screenings and applications, I was approved for the grant. I just had to find a house and close on it. I was grateful that two years prior that I paid off old collection debts and increased my credit score.

At that time, I knew nothing about real estate, buying houses, or what to even look for in a home. I hired a real estate agent and fired her. She did not have the time to show me homes. Hired a new real estate agent. This agent showed me lots of homes. I finally settled on a property that offered space for me to live and also rental investment property space. The building was a four-family flat that was converted into a duplex.

So the space was massive and had all of the features that I desired in a home in St. Louis, Missouri. It was owned by one of the City's elites from the Roberts Family. Since I was approved for an FHA loan, the building had to be ready to be moved in. There were a few issues with this property though: 1. Dampness and mold in the basement with his tenant. And 2. The foundation was not sound. There were thousands of dollars worth of remediation and repairs to be made and the buyer was only willing to contribute $1,000 to the cost. Ended up just letting that contract expire.

At that time, I was dating a man who owned over 50 properties in town. He is the landlord, managing, hiring staff for repairs and maintenance, collecting rent, etc. I traveled with him for many days as he took care of business regarding those properties. I watched him work long hours with many struggles and problems to solve. One day, he told me that his maintenance man told him that there was a property on Wells that the owner was looking to sell. The house was not on the market. Took a look at the outside of the property to size it up. It looked like a huge monstrosity or mansion sitting on a hill. I was impressed. Did not really survey the surrounding neighborhood in-depth.

We met with the owner of the building to discuss the selling price and set up an appointment for us to view all 4 2-bedroom apartments along with the basement. All I could see is dollar signs with their already being tenants in the building; I never considered all of the hard work that would come with being a landlord.

The seller and I came to an agreement on the selling price. My man Cedric wrote up the contract and we met at the local Starbucks to sign the contracts. I bought a building at a great price with no real experience. I closed the deal on August 16, 2016. That is the day, this little girl who has experienced so much trauma and even homelessness became not only a homeowner but a landlord and investor.

I was so grateful that my dreams had come true. I moved into my apartment a month later. That September, I dealt with my first major issue with the property because my tenant's furnace broke. This is when I realized that I did not have any resources to pull from to solve this problem. I called my man for suggestions on who to call and where to go. For the price that I paid for a used furnace and installation, in hindsight, I could have bought a new furnace. Because I ended up calling the installer back to the building several times regarding the used furnace.

The tenants were three BIPOC women who were all older than me. I believe they all resented me in some way for being the owner of their apartment building. They were used to paying this white man and were more comfortable with him. They talked to me badly. They stopped paying rent on time. They wanted extensions. Every day it seemed like someone had a new problem or something was breaking. The building did not originally pass the City's inspection.

There was work to do before they would pass the building. I just did not have the capacity to deal with the building but I trudged forward. Over time, one of the tenants that lived there for almost 20 years, moved out. Now, what was I going to do? For months, the apartment sat empty and in need of repair. I had no idea what the next steps were. "What do I do now?" is what I kept asking myself. Did not know where the funds would come from to actually do the work to make the apartment ready. There were so many different things to do. Replace the carpet, paint the walls, and update the bathroom and kitchen.

I was so overwhelmed. I always felt overwhelmed dealing with the building. Cried for so many days. I felt so alone. I knew people with properties but I could not bug them with my issues. Had to tough it out and figure things out. Now, I have not mentioned yet that I have bipolar depression which translates to days filled with a lack of focus and concentration, depression and days of not moving off the couch. Days of manic episodes or what I call rock star days where I think I can do EVERYTHING with no limits. I spend recklessly beyond my means. Staying up all night for days, creative juices flowing.

Mind racing a million ways. I was in St. Louis alone, an expat from Dallas, Texas. No relatives in town, just me and the created communities I was a part of. There were many lonely teary days where I was spinning out because of not knowing what to do. In hindsight, I could have sought out a mentor or people to assist me that had the experience instead of doing it all by myself. It is a hard road when you are a one-woman or one-man show. No support. No funding. No experience. Although this was my dream realized, it was also the biggest nightmare and the hardest thing I'd ever done. Being a landlord is not for the weak at heart.

To help me fix the vacant apartment, I enlisted the help of a stranger somewhat. It was not a great idea because not only did he move a drug dealer into my building. He set the deal up that the new tenant would be paying him rent and not me. I got the apartment fixed but it was not without a terrible cost. The new tenant was a total troublemaker with too many people coming to the apartment to deal with him. I noticed a car started sitting watching my building sitting in front of the building for hours. I even called the police on them but since they were the cops no one came to follow up. Eventually, this tenant left the building one night in a haste and left all of his belongings in the building for me to deal with.

One of the other tenants was always late and short with her rent. Then her gas was cut off for months and she had extension cords and electric heaters plugged up everywhere burning up all of the outlets. Then she moved a man into her unit without my permission and he refused to sign a new lease. She paid her rent late and short for the entire time that I owned the building. Finally, I threatened to evict her and we agreed that she would move.

Now the challenge was to find new tenants to fill the building back up. I listed the apartment in a few places and got calls from potential renters. I wanted quality tenants but needed to fill the apartment back up so I ended up taking people with bad rental histories.

Two new tenants visited the building and then put their deposits down for two apartments. There were things to fix in the two apartments. I would use the new tenants' deposits to fix those two apartments. I met a contractor at a gas station and after talking to him, I decided to hire him to fix several things in the apartment. Against my better judgment, I paid him the entire amount before any work was done because he insisted that he would need the funds to buy materials. I was scammed and lost over $2000 and he only installed a used hot water heater. He left some mismatched materials but that situation was a total loss.

The building did give me opportunities to hire other Black people and I am grateful for that. I hired a few Black people to do maintenance and assist with accounting and management. What I learned is that you must stay and watch the contractors as they do the work because they will either not do the job in its entirety or they will leave it a mess. One contractor actually tore up my apartment instead of fixing it. It was always a challenge to find someone who would legitimately do the work without any problems.

While I managed my building, I worked as an independent insurance agent for a year. That kept me busy setting appointments and visiting folks to write life insurance policies for them. It was very hard to focus on just doing one thing. The insurance work took my concentration away from dealing with the building. It stormed really bad one day and the roof started leaking. Then I found out that it cost $30,000 to replace the roof. It was one issue after another. Seemed like I was putting out fires daily. There were so many "fires" to put out it seemed like almost daily. The building whooped my butt.

The insurance business was really good to me during those years that I worked with a major brand. It was way more work as an Independent Agent. Everything was on me to do every step. It was very rewarding though knowing someone's family was protected if they died. People knew me in St. Louis as the "Insurance Lady" because I was always talking about insurance and passing out my cards.

While I owned the building, I started several businesses or business projects. One biz Be And Us LLC, came from a discussion that I had with a guy that I was dating. We were discussing starting t-shirt businesses. Where my brand name would be called "Be" and his brand would be "Us". In 2017, when I registered another LLC, I named the business Be And Us LLC. This name meant that if you are your best self and work together on common goals truly the dreams do work. We help each other to be great and successful. The plan was to use the brand to sell different original items that I created. One of the brand's first ventures was manufacturing Nigerian shea butter.

For starters, I started it with Shea butter. This sister on Facebook named Jessica had a Shea butter business and she talked about how she would get raw Shea butter from overseas and will package it.

One day I reached out to her and asked her about her Shea butter business and got her contact. Ended up purchasing 200 pounds of raw Nigerian shea butter. It cost a lot to ship the shea butter from Houston to St. Louis but I was willing to make the investment. It was a sight to see 200 pounds of raw Shea butter. I started a new system to whip the shea butter. Using a large pot and wooden spoon, I would stir the shea butter to make it smooth. Then I would put Shea butter into the mason jars and weigh them.

I wrote on the labels Be And Us LLC Nigerian Shea butter. To me, it was much better than the Ghanaian Shea butter that was already on the market. I sold this Shea butter at local community events within the St. Louis area. It was really awesome meeting people from various communities and backgrounds at these events. Really enjoyed talking with everyone, getting to know them and finding out what they are passionate about. Networking is my thing. I'm a real natural at connecting with people. People raged about the Shea butter and were repeat customers.

I gave out lots of samples of the shea butter to drum up business. People were loving the smooth silky feel of the Nigerian shea butter. The shea butter was sold at various locations in St. Louis and Philadelphia. I bought a total of 400 pounds of Shea butter then my distributor changed professions and stopped going home to visit Nigeria. That was the end of that business.

I would frequent Better Family Life for Master Teacher lectures like Ashra Kwesi, Dr. Richard D. King, M.D., Cress Francis Welding, Leonard Jeffries, Professor Griff, and so many more. One day, I heard Kaba Kamene AKA Booker T. Coleman. This was around the time of the unrest after Michael Brown, Jr. was murdered by Ferguson police officer Darren Wilson in 2014. Kaba Kamene suggested that instead of protesting, we could march to a local Black business, and everyone pledge to spend $25 each at the event.

I thought that was a great idea and began planning the event, the Ujamaa Cooperative Economics March from the only public African-centered school in the city, Pamoja Preparatory Academy at Cole to Progressive Emporium. This is one of the last Black bookstores in St. Louis. I organized a march for us to spend $25 each at the event. The event had Sponsors who provided a banner and catered the food for the event after the March. I enlisted the help of a few peers to have a drumline. The event brought in an additional $700 to Progressive Emporium in that one day. Also, I created t-shirts to commemorate the event that I sold until I ran out of them.

In the summer of 2017, I took two courses to learn Photoshop and beginner acrylic painting. Discovered that I really enjoyed painting a lot.

It was very relaxing and meditative. After class, I painted them and scanned the paintings to put the paintings on different merchandise on sites like Spring and Threadless. The artwork is on products like t-shirts, shower curtains and rug sets, notebooks, tote bags, mugs, stickers and so much more. This was an awesome expression of my creativity. This also led me to speak with my neighbor who collected Black art. I suggested to him that he put some of his original paintings on shower curtains so the Average Joe would have access to such a beautiful collection. He agreed and I started adding his collection of art to shower curtains and rug sets. These sets were very popular.

I submitted one of my paintings to a contest. My painting of a flower called "First Bloom" was selected by London's No Name Gallery's Challenge 21. And my painting is featured in their April 2021 magazine and YouTube channel. What an honor. Also, I started showcasing my art at art shows and community events.

My goals for going into business were to leave a legacy for my children, leverage my time, and produce something that allows my time to be free. For a year, I lived an entrepreneurial life with no job or boss. It was so great. Waking up doing whatever I wanted. Did not have a lot of money but I paid all of the building's bills and my personal bills with the income that the building brought in. I am very grateful for that time although hard, it gave me a taste of what freedom feels like. Another reason why I got in business was to help the plight of BIPOC people. Started partnering with other BIPOC businesses to sell their products.

Some of the brands that I worked with are Dail Chambers' Nu Mobile Healing and Yeyo Arts; selling everything she sold, like herbs, herbal teas, artwork, pins, jewelry, and a few of her books. Sold Raw Blends sweatshirts and the Buy Black Campaign's 100th Commemoration of the Massacre at Black Wall Street in Tulsa hoodies and t-shirts. One of my peers introduced me to the owner of Amber Book Store, Gregory Reed and the rest was history. I worked with him and his partner, our Ancestor Roland Younge to put their book inventory on their bookstore website. I redesigned their website (http://amberbookstores.com/) And I sold racks of books at the community events along with the other products. Grateful for the trust that these business owners put in me. Met and connected with so many wonderful people. Many of whom I am still friends with.

In 2018, I became an Independent Agent for Mutual of Omaha. That was a beast of another kind because there were many activities to do in order to be successful as an independent agent in the insurance industry. You must make a minimum of 100 calls per week to set up at least 20 appointments for the next week. Then you return any calls and call new leads. There is your own marketing to be done. Unlike working at an insurance agency at a household name company, they do the marketing for you.

All you have to do is pick up the phone and quote the potential client. Prepare for this week's appointments. Meetings with our team & Director during the week. Driving to all of these appointments. Waiting for clients. Dealing with lots of no-shows. Filling out applications. Submitting applications and collecting premiums. Follow-up appointments with clients whose policies were approved. Follow-up calls when payments are returned. I did all of this and more while managing the 4-Family Flat in the City of St. Louis. Kept me busy and it was a lot of hard work in those days. In hindsight, I would have hired a property manager and let no one know that I owned the property. Because the tenants' knowing that I was the owner tainted our relationship with each other.

In January 2019, I was working from home. On social media, I saw something about Nexcore Co-Working Space offering a week of free services in their space. Decided to take the offer to see if I'd be more productive out of the house. That week, I ran into my old boss Dana Kelly who was running her insurance & tax office out of the space. Met new entrepreneurs and talked to them about what we were each doing. One night, I went to one of their evening business classes about Podcasting. Did not have a podcast at the time though but I was curious. Years back, when I was in the insurance business, my good friend Dacia Polk told me to podcast on YouTube and show myself as an expert in the insurance industry.

Although a brilliant idea, I never started the podcast. On this night, one of the first things they asked us 8 that joined the class, was "What's the name of your podcast? And what is your podcast about?" Well, I did not have a podcast therefore, I made some stuff up on the fly. Called my podcast "News You Can Use Podcast." The premise was that mainstream media mostly show BIPOC people from a negative lens not highlighting the positivity happening within communities. The goal of the News You Can Use Podcast eventually evolved to giving

BIPOC business owners their proper "Shine" for their positive impact on the diaspora.

Allowing them to tell their business stories, and sharing their experiences of their business journey. Nexcore offered us studio time in their Podcasting Studio. Went home that night and wrote up what I wanted to say for my first podcast episode. Recorded about three hours of content that day on a range of topics while also highlighting some BIPOC brands and their events, and playing local artists and my friends' music.

The first several episodes of the podcast are of me talking about various topics from how breathing benefits you to Post-Traumatic Slave Syndrome. As things progressed, I would go on location to interview BIPOC business owners in St. Louis, Missouri. Interviewed artists, filmmakers, and authors and played positive music from BIPOC artists' submissions. Then I opened the podcast to the diaspora and recorded interviews on Zoom or Instagram. That is when A News You Can Use Podcast became an international podcast.

I have interviewed BIPOC business owners in Canada, the United Kingdom, England, Singapore, and mostly from the United States. The podcast streams wherever you stream your podcasts. Over 30 countries stream the podcast and over 5,000 downloads. There have been opportunities for brands to advertise on the podcast either through paid Sponsorships or some type of barter.

In 2019, I was restless and homesick. I'd been away from my mama and my hometown of Dallas, Texas for eight years. The City of St. Louis neighborhood off Martin Luther King Blvd. depressed me with all of its vagrancy and self-degradation. There was very little hope seen in this neighborhood where my property lay. After three years, the wear and tear of the responsibility of the building and the tenants had gotten to me. I was sorely tired and miserable. Had not enlisted the help of anyone to help me bear that burden. Talking with a friend, we discussed ways I get paid and see the world. The idea of teaching English overseas came up and I ran with that. Started researching programs and what to expect as far as salaries, Discovered some agencies who connected you to schools overseas.

I spoke with my sorority sister about her experience teaching English to Chinese children virtually. Ended up getting several contract offers including one from the Chinese Public School. Decided that I did not want to be in China wondering what is going on at the property here in the States. Therefore, I put the building on the market. We got a buyer after several showings. Working with a realtor, we contracted out to a female BIPOC contractor to paint the four apartments, remodel a bathroom, replace a steel column that held up the building in the basement, and do some other things around the apartment. I replaced the carpet in two apartments.

Replaced the hot water heater, and a refrigerator, and changed the outlets. There was so much to do to satisfy the buyer's loan request but we got everything done. On closing day, the buyer refused to sign the documents due to his Sovereign status therefore that deal did not go through. We obtained a second buyer. After signing all of the applications with his wife. At closing, he refused to sign the documents with his wife's name on them. Then, unfortunately, I foreclosed on the property and the two tenants were kicked out of the building by the bank.

Before the first closing day, I sold most of what I owned that I was not taking back home to Dallas, Texas. In June 2019, I drove my truck back home to be with my family and friends before I moved overseas to China in September 2019. Moved in with a friend, his wife, and his child. The two tenants that I obtained in May were mailing me their rent. The third tenant moved out in May and died the day she moved into her new apartment. While I was in Dallas, I visited my mama and enjoyed myself but I stopped paying the bills at my property in St. Louis. Stopped paying the mortgage.

You see, bipolar sometimes has a way of helping/making me blow money and not be responsible with it. I lost the property before we could find a solid buyer for the property. (Shhh. Don't tell my mama) In hindsight, I should still be on the property today and have some managing it as a property manager. I let a great thing get away but you live and learn, right? I did learn a lot about myself. I never want to be a landlord again. Get a property manager. And I do not need to have a big house for myself, I am comfortable with a 1500 sq. ft. home. Lastly, I know so much about homes now.

As the time drew near for me to leave to go to China, I grew more and more nervous anticipating what the culture and foods would be like. Wondering if I would say the wrong thing to the wrong person and be locked up in a Chinese jail indefinitely. Some of my peers started sending me online articles about Americans being banned from leaving China. I was scared now all of my boldness, determination, and tenacity faded away. I did not want to go anymore. Plus my mama was getting nauseous quite often having "sick spells." Ultimately, I decided to not go to China and teach English. It was very important to me that I stay home and take care of my mama as she aged. She needed me.

Did not know how right I was.... During this time, my mama's boyfriend and best friend was fighting for his life with Cancer. She was nursing him. He died in Feb. 2020. Within that same week, my mama had a heart attack. I believe from a broken heart. This was during the time I would have been in China had I chosen to go. I was able to take her to the hospital and stay with her at the hospital for the few days she was admitted. And I am grateful to be with my mama to care for her, run her errands and drive her to places. Because when I was in St. Louis for all of that time, I missed her so much and I did not see her often enough. Secondly, the other reason I am glad that I did not go to China is that the Coronavirus Covid 19 erupted in China first. And they were not letting BIPOC citizens out of the country. I am so fortunate that

I am in tune with myself and at that time, I listened to my gut, my instincts, and my first mind.

With Covid 19 came the lockdown in March 2020 here in Dallas. Did not like the idea of being "caged up" in the apartment. When that happened I did more gig work with the rideshare delivering groceries and food from restaurants. My business was thriving and making sales at in-person events in St. Louis. But the people that I grew up with here in Dallas, did not know me as an entrepreneur. And because of the 'Rona, there were not any vendor community events to attend. I had to convert my business to an online business by putting my products on a site. Still have not mastered the eCommerce business. At that time, I was selling Stephen Cutt's Buy Black Campaign's 100th Commemoration of Tulsa's Black Wall Street Massacre hoodies and t-shirts. Selling silver plated necklaces and gold overlay silver plated necklaces along with jade bracelets.

Started selling my original acrylic paintings and the collections of designs from the paintings on Threadless. Sold a few of the masks designed with my paintings on them. And I was still selling the shower curtains and rug sets with my friend's collection of Black art on them.

During the winter of 2019 in December, I had a vivid dream, where Tory Russell, my activist peer, was telling me that I had not done enough to let my children know that I still loved them. What was so strange about the dream was that I usually do not remember dreams or even have dreams at all. I was so jolted from the dream that I penned the first edition of my first children's book Mommy & Daddy Do You Still Love Me Anymore? In one day. The book was unedited and had no illustrations.

The only picture was a picture of my children, my mama, and me at Chuck E Cheese. The book was written as a love letter to my 4 children with a universal message of hope to any child or adult who experienced foster care and/or adoption. Did not get very many sales but I pressed on. Two years later in the summer of 2021, I published the 2nd Ed. edited with illustrations by my good friend Dail Chambers as a paperback and an ebook. The audiobook of the book has also been produced in 2022.

The 2nd Ed. of the children's book was submitted for the Spring 2022 Book Fest Awards and won Honorable Mention in the Nonfiction Family genre. This time I pivoted my business to feature my writing and my speaking abilities. I still have my original designs from my original paintings available for purchase on Spring and Threadless but I do not market them. I have shifted to become an Author, now an Award-winning Author. Through emailing bookstores and influencers my books are available near and far. The books are available for purchase and check out at several brick-and-mortar locations, libraries, and online.

Featured on Turn the Pages, Black Children's Books and Authors What's Your Story?, Shoutout DFW, and VoyageATL Magazine. The

Cover of Huami Magazine. Amazing riveting review by Lauren Simone Publishing House Publisher Dr. Melissa Sue John. I have appeared on at least 40 Podcasts and Radio Shows since writing my books.

In the summer of 2021, I collaborated with the Visionary Dr. Vernessa Blackwell to write one of the chapters in the #1 Best-Selling book Finding Joy in the Journey Vol. 2: Healthy Ways to Find Joy During Difficult Times 90 Day Devotional. 90 different Authors wrote a chapter for this anthology. This was a different type of project from my children's books. This was another way though for me to encourage, inspire and motivate. It was fun to write and did not take very long to write. Vernessa walked us through every publishing step and was very knowledgeable about the process. That same year, I also told my Pandemic story in Angie Bee Production's audiobook series The Single, Saved, Struggle: The Struggle Continues. I wrote about some of my experiences during the Coronavirus Pandemic along with 7 other Authors. Then Angie Bee narrated all of our stories. Angie Bee was also a Co-Author in the Finding Joy anthology.

At the end of 2021, I agreed to be a Co-Author for Singapore's Viki Esther Cheng's Gold Nuggets for Entrepreneurs international anthology. I wrote a chapter about the history of Black businesses in America. Telling some of the struggles of a Black business owners here in America. Also shared a plethora of advice and resources for any business owner to succeed that I have learned from my experiences in business. Viki Esther and I "met" online on Facebook as Podcasters in 2020. We were on each other's podcasts. Gold Nuggets for Entrepreneurs will be published later this year.

In conclusion, my experiences in business have been rocky with some successes. It was a hard road but I am grateful that I took it. Next year, I hope to host several book events and to have my book distributed in more bookstores. I am grateful for every lesson learned.

I have been chosen as 1 of 30 BIPOC business owners for the Truist Scale Up Initiative with The Dec Network where I will receive mentoring and coaching, marketing campaigns, the Mayor's startup package, and connections to funding. I am so grateful for this opportunity to learn to grow my business and work with other professionals. My journey is filled with ups and downs. My friend calls me "Do It All". I am creative and I love to enact my so-called good ideas. I take risks and might need to do more research. Hope that my life inspires and motivates my children to dream big and maybe others too. But I won't die with any regrets and that is what I am most grateful for.

Bit.ly/FrenchyBooks
Linktr.ee/FrenchaireG
Facebook.com/FrenchaireGardner
Instagram.com/Frenchaire_Gardner
Twitter.com/msfrenchy06
Pinterest.com/FrenchysWonders
https://www.tiktok.com/@frenchaire?_t=8YcziVFLE0E&_r=1

Chapter II: Lesley Ventura-Lessons Learned

"Life is what you make of it."

Having Business Partners

Going into business with family

Some people say that you should not go into business with family members. That there are more cons than pros when going into business with family. While that may be true for others. I believe the opposite. I'd like to tell my story circling around working with a business partner. Whether it's a family member, friend, acquaintance, etc, the principles are similar.

In most cases, working with family could be a disaster waiting to happen. But in my case, I am in business with my partner in life and we made it work. In this chapter, I am sharing with you my business journey with my husband along with our successes, struggles and learnings along the way.

When I'm reading something, It's very important for me to have takeaways from it. My hope is that, in reading this chapter, you find at least a nugget or 2 that may be helpful not only for your business, but also in your personal life. Also, I hope it serves as an inspiration for you to keep moving forward in your business.

Lesson # 1: Finding the right business partner that compliments you

When we first met

My husband and I are entrepreneurs at heart. The fact that we were both already interested in business prior to knowing each other is what drew us closer to each other. While we may have our differences, our outlook in life is the same. We both want the same for our future. The right business partner can make or break a business. When finding a business partner, the most important thing is that you find someone you can trust. It is very important for all of the parties involved to look out for each other, have each other's back and genuinely commit to the business.

Lesson # 2 Embrace your differences.

My husband and I could not be more different. My husband is more of the risk taker, action type of guy and wants things done now. I'm more cautious, more analytical but take longer to take action. But in business, you need both personalities. While we are completely different personality wise, he compliments me when it comes to business. His strengths are my weakness and my strengths are his weakness.

We also think differently. In business, there's value in thinking differently. Not only does it give you more ideas to bounce off each other, it allows you to look at situations from different angles. You just have to learn how to put your ego in your pocket when necessary.

Lesson # 3: Know your Market

When I met my husband, he had an online printing business while working a full time job. I started helping out also while working a full time job. As the business grew, it became overwhelming. Since we both didn't have the time to immerse ourselves in the business to learn the ropes, he decided to sell the online business. That was the beginning of the dot com boom and we failed to see the vast market for online business. In retrospect, we should have kept the business, learned the ropes and grown it bigger knowing what we know now. After selling the business, we took a hiatus and focused more on our personal lives. 3 years later, we tied the knot.

Lesson # 4: Have a vision

Prior to getting married, we were very conscious about our appearance. However, since getting married, we started gaining weight! We decided to start our health and wellness quest to lose weight and feel better about ourselves. We found this cleansing program and personally combined it with nutrition, fitness and alkaline water.

We had such great success on the program personally that we decided to share this success with others by packaging it to sell to clients.

Our vision was to share our program to people who want to not only lose weight but also lead healthier lives. Through proper nutrition and hydration as well as fitness, not only do we achieve a healthier mind and body, we also lose weight and look good in the process.

Lesson # 5: Do one thing and do it right.

"This is so true when it comes to business. Ideally you pick one thing that you are good at and capitalize on that. Having too many moving parts dilutes your focus."

Over the course of months, we found that although the program worked, it had too many moving parts that it was hard to manage. Our solution was to hone in on one part and focus on it. We looked at the full program carefully and found potential in the alkaline water. The fact that our clients just kept coming back for the alkaline water solidified our decision. Furthermore, the alkaline water really helped my husband deal with his acid reflux.

This time, we focused on selling the alkaline machines. The machines were pricey and we decided to install them for our clients as an added service. Because of the installation part, it quickly became a maintenance and repair service. That was not exactly the vision we wanted for the business. So we asked ourselves, what if we could bottle the water and sell it in stores for cheaper?

QURE, Alkaline Bottled Water

Back then, it was unheard of to bottle alkaline water. Yes, there were a few brands already out in the market. However, after doing our research, we found that they're not even alkaline in the bottle - since alkalinity in water was not retained in bottle containers. My husband, who has expertise in processes in the petrochemical industry, spent months doing research and found the perfect process to be able to retain the alkalinity in the water. We created a proprietary process that mimics Mother Nature's hydrologic cycle. My husband invented the machine which involved quring of ionic minerals in water not only for the alkalinity properties but also to create a silky smooth tasting water. After months of research, testing, trial and error and sourcing of the right blend of minerals, QURE was born.

So, what is QURE Water?

QURE® is simply: smooth tasting, pristine, clean hydration. With its nature inspired alkaline process, it is uniquely infused with traces of naturally-occurring ionic alkaline minerals and electrolytes with a powerful high pH of 10. Its super-hydrating nature is designed to Refresh, Renew, and Revitalize your body.

Whole Foods Journey plus more Stores

QURE was first introduced in Whole Foods and quickly gained traction. Because of its unique features and of course, the silky smooth taste, it was a favorite among Hollywood celebrities and Athletes. We were also featured in various publications such as People and US Weekly Magazine. With the help of a broker, we went from just Whole Foods to more specialty grocery stores and restaurants in Southern California to eventually Sprouts. We were slowly becoming a well known brand in the West, even becoming the top 3 alkaline water in Nielsen Rating.

Lesson # 6: Pick the right business relationships (customers, vendors, contractors, etc.)

As our business grew, we encountered issues with production not being able to keep up causing delays in fulfillment. Instead of focusing on our sales growth, we had to divert and try to look for vendors that can help us sustain the growth. This distracted us from the momentum that we already created.

In business, just like in life, relationships are very important. You want relationships that last and grow with you. Once you pick the right business relationships, it is also very important to nurture those relationships.

Lesson # 7: Stay Focus

Another distraction was - believe it or not - a lot of opportunities that came our way with the success of the business. Don't get me wrong, opportunities are good. It's also very important to pursue the ones that matter. While there were opportunities that helped us with our business, there were also opportunities that distracted us from the main business. Unfortunately for us, we sometimes momentarily lost sight of our focus and entertained a lot of opportunities that slowed down our growth.

Lesson # 8: Pace yourself

Expand at the right time, expand when you have the funding or the plans for funding.

National Expansion with a Master Distributor

One of those opportunities that came with the success was for national expansion with a master distributor. We got enamored about the possibilities and partnered up with the master distributor to take on national distribution of the Brand. We failed to see the red flags. This master distributor did not really have a lot of reach in the West but strong in the East. We were used as a catapult for them to expand their business in the West, diluting our efforts in the process. This was by far one of our many biggest mistakes to date.

Lesson # 9: Know your numbers and do not compromise your margins.

To fit the master distributor, we had to significantly reduce our margins. Due to limited funding and eroding margins, This did not allow us to focus on solidifying a brand in our home turf. Instead, our efforts were now focused on building a machine in the East Coast for the expansion. Furthermore, the price of the product became so high that it was no longer competitive and we were losing money everytime we promoted. So we reduced our promotional spend. Another Mistake. With other competitor brands getting funding to increase promotional spend, we were now slowly starting to lose our strong foothold.

In retrospect, what we could have done was raise funding to cover the expansion or cut off ties sooner with the distributor and promote,promote, promote.

Lesson # 10: Monitor, Monitor, Monitor.

VP of Sales, Broker Network and COVID

Once we finally had the guts to cut off ties with the master distributor, we hired a VP of Sales to do the transition who in turn hired brokers. While this is not a bad move at all, it was definitely a failure on our end to monitor the performance of the VP of Sales. We failed to constantly monitor the poor sales performance of our sales support. With more competitors in the industry, we could not afford a poor sales performance. That being said:

Lesson # 11: Fire Fast

When people you partner up with do not give you the results that you agreed on within a specified time frame, you need to be able to get rid of them fast and find someone who can deliver the results that you need. This might sound ruthless but we have been burned so many times before by being too nice that at some point you have to weigh in what's more important for the business. Otherwise, there might be no more business to save.

Lesson # 12: Be nimble

COVID and Onwards

...And then COVID hit. While we were still reeling on the missteps that we took in the business, it is now harder to compete. We had to pivot - FAST. One of the advantages of being a small business is you can make strategic moves faster than big companies.

QURE Power Launch

The whole industry is now starting to change with Covid. Additionally with the pressures of plastic packaging, we wanted to pivot and create a product that is more environmentally friendly and with more added function to the product.- primarily selling directly to customers.

We decided to create the **ONLY** highly soluble line of powdered nutritional hydration alkaline mix with delicious flavor essences that you add to your water to power up your body's natural functions - focusing on sleep, mental boost, skin glow and endurance.

After a year in R&D, we finally developed and launched QURE POWER in late 2022 - a soluble alkaline drink that can transform any boring water into a 9 pH alkaline water with nutritional goodness, such as vitamins, minerals, antioxidants and electrolytes with delicious essence of flavors, specifically curated to support the body's healthy functions such as:

- Better, Deeper sleep -
- 4 Hour Mental Focus
- Beautiful Glowing Skin In 15 Days
- Physical Endurance and Athletic Performance

In a nutshell, QUREPOWER powers up your hydration with alkaline antioxidant health function-specific Nutritionals alkalized to be easy and soothing to your stomach.

Lesson # 13: Never Give Up

As you have read so far, nothing in our business journey came easy. It has been full of ups and downs. 'Should haves' and 'Could haves' are endless at this point. The most important thing to remember is that we learn from our mistakes and grow from our experiences.I remember this quote that I've heard before (I can't remember where I heard it from): "If we're not growing, we're dying."

As entrepreneurs, our lives will always be full of the challenges and struggles along with our successes. It's a seesaw of emotions most of the time. Most entrepreneurs are just good at managing or perhaps hiding it. But that's what makes us different - because we love what we do and we will always pursue our dreams, we go on. One of the important ingredients of an entrepreneur is grit. Grit allows us to have the mental strength to hold on and never give up.

Still here and fighting - together -

What helps me in this journey is the fact that my husband and I are in this together.

Usually, the road to business is a lonely journey. Having a business partner makes it, in my opinion, more manageable. You become each other's strengths. I honestly believe that having my husband as my business partner has made this journey much more fulfilling. We share and enjoy the successes together. We go through the challenges together. Success becomes sweeter and challenges become more achievable.

I'm not going to lie, this road to entrepreneurship with my husband is definitely not easy. Sure there are fights - what matters is making sure that the 'fights' about the business can be repurposed to productive discussions that reach a decision to move forward. Sometimes, in order to achieve that, arguments are inevitable. How you deal with your differences is what matters.

Always move forward.

Make sure that both of you are constantly improving and growing in business as well as in personal life. In truth, this is not only for husband and wife partnership in business. This goes for all other relationships, not only in your business but also in all other aspects in life.

To my partner in life and in business, I love you always. With you by my side, I know we will always make it no matter what. Thank you for being my strength.

Company name: QURE
website: www.qurewater.com[1]
Facebook: @qurewater
Instagram: @qurewater

---

1.   http://www.qurewater.com/

Chapter III: Zarinah Hameen- Beginnings are Scary

"Beginnings are usually scary, endings are usually sad, but it's what's in the middle that counts. So when you find yourself at the beginning, just give hope a chance to float up. And it will." - Steven Rogers

Though it's my favorite quote, I would state that as it pertains to business, Beginnings are usually inconsistent. It's full of inspiration, experimentation and the excitement of a thought transitioning into a dream, turning that dream into an action, and finally watching it come to life to proudly watch it grow.

However, beginnings at times feel one-sided, but with everything there's the balance of uncertainty, especially during the process of turning a dream into a successful "career" choice. For me, those were the good ole days, becoming an entrepreneur and starting my own business or so I thought at the time.

To date, I'm the CEO of an award-winning company and as its leader, I was named "Marketing and Advertising CEO of the Year" by CV Magazine for 2017. In 2022, we were inducted into the Marquis Who's Who in America, the company was awarded the Philadelphia Award for Business and Consulting and one of our Podcasts was rated #13 of the "Top 90" Podcasts for Black Wealth and Finance by FeedSpot. In addition, the company was also nominated for a 2017 WeWork Creator award for innovation, a 2018 Grant Recipient for the Grow with Google Challenge Program, and in 2019 was nominated as a company to watch by Philadelphia Magazine.

Though I don't care much about accolades, I had a mentor once tell me that they are best used for status and not recognition. The strength of that recognition brings on the best opportunities. You don't want to design a business to receive accolades but while building or creating a startup, look for opportunities where you can obtain them.

In 2020, my company was accepted into the SheaMoisture's Women of Color E-Learning Hub, Spectrum Reach's Rebound Program, and Goldman Sachs 10,000 Small Businesses Program. Accolades are like getting a college degree or entering a certificate program, it's not about the education itself, but the document of completion. You took the time to work hard and get it. That's why we live in a society where a college degree once ensured more jobs than just a high school diploma.

She was right. I'm truly thankful for what happened once, the awards started pouring in. My company had the pleasure of working with the SuperBowl Committee during the 2018 NFL SuperBowl in Minneapolis, Minnesota and as a true Philly girl and die-hard Eagles Fan, the biggest reward was witnessing my team conquer their first SuperBowl win in Franchise History!

Right after receiving the award from CV Magazine and WeWork in 2017, I got to represent our brand by attending some of the most amazing conferences in the Tech industry, from The Grace Hopper Conference, fully funded by Google, The Women in Product conference hosted by a few small names such as Facebook, Twitter, Linkedin, and pretty much all of Silicon Valley, all the way to an exclusive conference with only 75 attendees, hosted by SnapChat (I'm not allowed to ever discuss the details of this conference since we had to sign an NDA upon arrival).

As I write this chapter, it's serving as a much needed distraction for preparing a speech for the Podfest Summit, which kicks off at the end of the week. I was approached by the Founders to inspire attendees on successful podcasting and branding.

Not to single out one experience over any of the others, but as I said earlier, always balance business with the perks and enjoyment of ownership. The most memorable experience didn't take place at the conference itself but while attending The Grace Hopper Conference, on the third night, a few of us were invited and bused to Disney World in the middle of the night (not knowing at the time that Google had rented out the entire park just for us to party and ride the rides, uninterrupted).

It started with a blow out party at The Epcot Center, followed by 3 hours of riding all the rides we could muster in the park until 3am with the only outside interactions being the poor workers who stayed late to truly make it our Disney (World)! Thank you, Google.

However, circling back to the beginning, my biggest dilemma was simply deciding on what area or industry to focus on. My greatest accomplishment at that time was when I figured it out (Again, or so I thought). I spent my career working in the non-profit sector in business development for several non-profit organizations, most notably was the Headquarters of Goodwill Industries International.

I worked in donor relations, fundraising, presentation/public speaking, webinar/content creation, family strengthening, education initiatives, but mostly as a grant writer. Through the course of that career I secured over 190 million dollars for charities and support systems for marginalized communities.

My biggest passion is or should I say, I was born to be a writer. I don't consider it a skill, being a writer is a gift and purpose. The idea of creating content and using it to indirectly affect millions of people through my efforts made grants management the easiest choice I've ever made.

However, I also loved the tech industry and quickly became an expert in website and mobile design/development, digital marketing, lead generation, seo/ppc, and software programming. I was able to be equally effective in that industry as well. Honestly though, besides the work itself, the two industries have similar missions.

Being a professional writer and a tech guru I was accomplishing the same outcome: Big ideas transferred through content and creation that leads to fruition or should I say, a finished product. It requires thought, detailed process, and implementing a design of a product that garners the attention of its audience. It made perfect sense to me that I was attracted to both.

In the beginning, I decided to focus on professional writing services because this was at a time where I hadn't made the connection between the two and thought I had to choose one. In 2013, I was entering my 5th year of living in Washington DC, so it seemed appropriate to incorporate my company and name it, Capitol Hill Writing and Consultation.

In order to make this "dream" a reality, it took a lot of cutting down on my life and living expenses. So, shortly after starting the business in Washington DC, two months later, I moved back home to Philadelphia. This was definitely a strategy move. If you've never lived in DC, most of us who have would tell you that it's a city of non-natives and opportunists.

Now I've realized that even though I was still building my own empire, I was still being inconsistent and trying to find my way. I ended up taking a few years to travel, mostly Europe and Africa. I was also dealing with the death of my Father and thought it best to put my own passions on hold and honor his memory by taking over his company.

When I reflect, I wasn't really following my "dreams" but his and in taking that time away, I was able to see clearly what he would have wanted for me but also what I truly wanted (a pandemic/quarantine will do that to you)! As a result, in 2021, I returned, with a new mission, future goals and finally knowing EXACTLY what made sense for myself and legacy. I officially established Au'loni Media Group, LLC.[1] It was the perfect company to combine all of my passions under one umbrella of support and services.

In just the last year since its official inception, Au'loni Media Group, LLC was selected for a 2022 Philadelphia Award[2] in the areas of Business and Coaching and inducted into The Philadelphia Media Founder's Exchange with The Lenfest Institute of Journalism[3]. Our podcast #BlackWealthIsBack[4] was selected as one of the top 80 podcasts on the internet for "BlackWealth and Finance" by Feedspot [5]in 2022 and in 2021, Our Podcast, Disrupt Tech[6] was a speaker at the

---

1. http://www.amgroupllc.biz

2. https://philadelphia.areadvise.com/PressReleaseub.aspx?cc=DMNP-YBFR-JUXX&fbclid=IwAR2X2VuHX37QLQmLRT6Ljs1wvNM18jcKB-pCeXfsPVG4xLJvThNXVINmyPo

3. https://www.lenfestinstitute.org/

4. http://www.anchor.fm/blackwealthisback

5. https://blog.feedspot.com/black_wealth_and_investing_podcasts/?fbclid=IwAR0tyHsVj3BUQZjp8JdG1exj2Z06knoePKIzylA5pBrpkI4Vyhl92X9HnL8

6. http://www.anchor.fm/disrupt-tech

International Podfest Summit[7] that later went on to break the Guinness World Records for most attendees to participate in a podcast summit.

We focus on merging traditional media with modern technology. Through Broadcast, Digital, and Print Media, we minimize the gatekeeper's influence over the voice of the underrepresented and disenfranchised, to better strengthen our global community.

On June 4, 2022, I celebrated 9 years of business and it's been the most terrifying, unstable, inconsistent, yet, amazing, exhilarating, and rewarding experiences of my life! Choose your poison. But just know, until you take a risk in life, you never really know who you are. Decide.

Website: www.amgroupllc.biz[8]

Facebook: @aulonimedia

Instagram: @auloni_meda_group

---

7.   https://scontent-iad3-1.xx.fbcdn.net/v/t1.6435-9/
147841048_880210482740723_7218641384092446133_n.jpg?_nc_cat=103&ccb=1-7&_nc
_sid=8bfeb9&_nc_eui2=AeEOdcO_4CR86N1WZTnlHHq4QkEtMaEIZltCQS0xoQhmW1
xx7a84VeTTpZCwjcT9SZc&_nc_ohc=Wbgv5VzzTq0AX-_Qux5&_nc_ht=scontent-iad3-1.xx
&oh=00_AT9kXXCCIDldZK7HhKr_-FGS-qXnKPGkXmUDUf_3sDB8ag&oe=62E7BAC
B

8.   http://www.amgroupllc.biz

Chapter IV: Chhavi Jain-It's About Perspective

"All that we see or seem is but a dream within a dream." — *Edgar Allan Poe*

CEO & Founder Live AI Dream

My journey as a startup owner is nothing less than a roller coaster ride but the ride I loved the most so far. The experience, passion, energy, internal growth, realizing self-weaknesses, strengths, inhibitions, blind spots, looking at things from different perspectives, finding group of supporters/advisors, planning while keeping several distinct aspects of business in mind, taking feedback and feeling gratitude for people who provide knowledge and support along the way is just far beyond my expectations. And something that is invaluable.

I have been dreaming of starting my own company since I was in the 6th grade. My reason and purpose have always been to leave behind my legacy and to contribute to science while I live. However, as a kid the concept was not crystal clear to me, but I always envisioned a pharmacy store where poor people can get medicine for free, and which is funded by my highly successful company. But that being said this vision has kept me on my toes and along with my studies I took part in several different activities, competitions and tried to work on my language skills, (understanding different aspects of how to be a more attentive listener and persuasive communicator).

I tried to network as much as possible in every situation and organized several different types of social gatherings and events whenever possible to learn more about working in different situations, where I don't have any authority or free flow of money and a very slight margin of error (being a very pampered kid from middle class family none of these situations were comfortable for me).

But with time I started putting myself in situations that I knew would be a good learning opportunity and would really make me feel uncomfortable. I believe that whenever we are uncomfortable, and we can manage our emotions and fears, we get the ability to learn much more quickly and those learnings stay with us for a much longer time because we have really put our heart and soul in the work. And the benefit of all this was I got from the President of India, Chief minister of my state, my name was published in several newspapers for my academic achievements, and I stayed in the top four rankers throughout my education.

But since I had no idea about how to set up my own software company and my friends also mostly were preparing for interviews in multinational companies. So I also ended up joining a multinational company and I feel at the time I did not have the resources, experience or ecosystem to establish my own company so it was the right thing to do. But little did I know that because of my habits of multitasking and participating in many different activities and contributing to critical projects, I started getting awarded with quick salary increases, hefty bonuses and unique opportunities.

But I used to find myself very often in a situation where I am the only woman in meetings, sometimes only women in my team and sometimes only women in a particular role or entire department. This gave me a feeling of restlessness, so I started working for women's causes, started talking to many different female employees first within the company, then within the industry and then even to students. And everywhere I found the same pattern that women representation was always less. There were very few examples of women researchers, women speakers and even women employees in new and cutting-edge technologies.

Many women employees or researchers used to share stories of bias. So, I started participating in and leading women groups and leadership panels. I started realizing that when I set up some group from scratch, get it going from grounds up and make it successful then it gives me a very different type of satisfaction, the satisfaction that I never feel otherwise and if it creates a positive impact on someone's life and if I get a verifiable result or feedback about it then it makes me feel even more purposeful and happy in life while materialistically if I buy something or do something luxurious and get some social status out of it then it feels temporary and sometimes even empty.

Again, that entrepreneurship thought started coming in my mind very actively again after setting up many different groups and organizations successfully (for companies owned by other people). Even in my technical work I often found myself selecting the work that is not clearly defined, in a very early stage almost just a two-liner idea and then taking that idea and shaping it into a real product that millions of customers use under very renowned brand names used to make me extremely happy.

However, if the project is very well structured, have sometimes even extra resources allocated to it then I found myself craving for more fulfilling roles where I can architect the system from scratch, talk to different stakeholders, establish clear interfaces, clear responsibilities, and do all the task planning and eventually make sure everything goes on time with a very well tested product.

I did this for many years successfully for different projects and then again started evaluating should I start my own company now. But after researching some more, I realized I was an expert in the field where huge initial setup cost is involved, and margin per product is small however the business model is more in small profit from huge customer base. Also, hiring more people in that space was like finding a needle in a haystack. As a first-time startup owner it felt almost impossible.

At that time, I started feeling the need of upskilling myself and to gain understanding of other technologies as well. I wanted to gain an understanding of some industry that is based on innovative technology, less crowded space so that startups are possible even with small investment.

With these specifications in mind, I could narrow down to three technologies in my case it was blockchain, stock market (or financial analysis tools) and artificial intelligence. I took a few week courses for all three of them and realized that I absolutely love artificial intelligence. I loved it to the point that I wanted to work only in artificial intelligence (AI). But making a career transition from successful and seasoned telecom RF professional to AI professional was a daunting task because everything was different about these areas and there are still very few people who know both the areas simply because the overlap is very small.

But I was not ready to give up. I started doing my masters in artificial intelligence and joined a different group where I could get an artificial intelligence related role till I figured out what exactly I love to do in the artificial intelligence space. But one thing was clear to me that I did not want to leave my job and start my company without a deep understanding about the technology and different areas and market for the technology. So, I started putting my heart and soul in learning this modern technology and working on it. And started narrowing down on the specific topics and areas that would be a highly successful area for well executed startups in future. In the process I became global women lead of tinyML (a non-profit organization highly active in the space) along with becoming AI research manager for a very renowned multinational company.

So again, the choice between good enough paycheck, social status, and the autonomy to make

small decisions while still protected from the high risk of starting my own company started taking me towards continuing in the job for some more time at least. But it was as if my unconscious mind always knew what I should be doing.

While I was not consciously crafting my path, I started getting this thought every single day that if I would not set up my own company now then I would never be able to know "what if I tried it". And this thought started coming to my mind from once in a day to thrice in a day, and then it changed into constant parallel thought in my mind. I started evaluating what is the risk and what is the gain in continuing in the job versus trying to set up my own business.

The risk of leaving the job was very clear and things that were at stake were financial security, social status that is associated to my job title in a very well-known company, perceived power by society since I was also doing people management, recruitment, giving presentations on well-known platforms, going to prestigious conferences and more than that I had a working support system around me that I crafted during so many years of working for the same company and in the same city.

However, the things that were at stake if I never left that job and started my own company were a big potential lifetime regret – "what if I tried setting up my own company".

Not even trying to do what I wanted to do for many years and potential impact on the society that I can make if my company becomes successful, setting up a path for other women engineers and girl child, that they can also navigate, ability to experience something so unique that no one can buy with money, leaving legacy for my child and having a platform where i can keep contributing and where I don't ever have to retire. As a company owner I probably will be able to retain the entire social circle that I built through my years of hard work even after a certain age.

While if I continue working for some other company once an employee retires people mostly start getting out of touch. While as an owner if we treat our employees right, partners respectfully and set up a system that constantly gives back to society then it is easier to retain the social circle and even grow it with time.

So, the choice was clear, either taking risks when I still have a lot of energy and motivation to work. Or regretting later when I cannot do anything about it. I realized that I needed less

things to live and I wanted many more happy memories when I die. So, I felt compelled to take a leap of faith and start on my journey of setting up my own company.

Ah, although I prepared for it for so long, the feelings, the mental strength, the overwhelming emotions, constant need of learning, growing more, finding new things about our own personality, those are the things that no preparation, no course, and no storyteller can ever communicate properly. If you already had your first child then maybe I can say that it is very similar to holding your first child for the very first time in your hands.

The sudden burst of emotions all sorts of emotions happiness that is so unique, sense of

getting something that is extremely invaluable, feeling of fulfillment as if something was missing the whole time and now we know that it is complete. The sense of responsibility that we have to make it successful and it is going to represent who we truly are and to raise it in a manner that we can feel proud of.

At the same time, fear of the unknown, do we have all the skills to make it grow? Who will support and provide correct guidance when needed? How will we manage so much work? Would we be able to do justice to it and how to change our daily schedule and leave those old habits that are a constant part of our daily schedule till now? The old friends who are still unmarried (in this case who are still working as salaried employees) would they still be part of our life as much as they were earlier and if not how will we stop missing them and would they perceive us in the same way as they used to?

So a major part of starting up your own company consists of mental strength, organizing thoughts, promise to grow, learn and improve every single day, face rejection so many times and so many ways that the ego vanishes and only self-esteem stays. The ability to take feedback constantly, getting out in the world, and putting yourself at the risk of failure every single day. Also, taking actions that may never bear fruit and need a lot of effort and using money and time in the most judicious way. Here are the five things that I feel I have learnt and i need to constantly follow as a startup owner

(1) Look at the long game plan and don't try to rush into choices that may give financial returns in the short term but throw us on a self-sabotaging path in the long run.

One example of it is hiring employees for full time instead of outsourcing work to freelancers. Since full-time employees are usually cheaper from a monthly salary perspective. However, if the company doesn't have enough runway yet, then we can't be sure what will happen tomorrow so any such decision affects not just your company's reputation but also families who depend on you to provide for their monthly expenses.

Don't rush into hiring full time employees. Hire contractors or freelancers initially.

(2) As a startup, be flexible, the day that we start a company with this brilliant idea of a very critical market use case which we can solve. And when we actually launch our first product in the market should be at least a few weeks to a few months apart in most of the cases. Instead of sitting and working on technical problems in that time period, divide your time judiciously and before working on full-fledged product work on just a demo product, collect feedback from the market as many times and as much as possible.

Collecting feedback from family, from friends and from the market all have different benefits and different risks so be aware of it. Family and friends usually have biased opinions about us so the opinion about products also gets colored with that bias.

However, the market will usually judge only the product but once we launch demo product in market we are not just collecting feedback, but we are also conveying information to our intended recipients (potential customers) but also unintended recipients (potential competitors) so be aware and careful about it.

(3) Having at least few experienced advisors around is extremely beneficial because as a startup founder we don't know what we don't know. So many things that are in our blind spot are very obvious to other people who have experience with working with startups as VCs, founders or employees

(4) Try to legally protect business and yourself from day one, register the company with the right type, follow correct ethical practices, follow guidelines, license terms and put proper NDAs, copyrights, trademarks and patents in place before sharing ideas.

(5) Don't jump at the first investment that you can potentially receive, be very careful with this aspect. Different phases of business have different negotiation power, getting investment in the idea stage is very costly both in terms of time and in terms of stake in the company. Once we have a demo product then it is different and once we have a successful revenue generating product then it is different. The more mature stage the business is in the more power we have to select the correct investor with better hold on company equity.

However, it all depends on how much money we can invest in business without getting investment from other channels and if the choice is between not being able to start versus starting with a lower percentage stake in the company then later is better. Also, a team from an investor's team can also have a significant impact on the company and even the founding team. If values are aligned and if investors have experience in the same space then it could be an advantage.

(6) Selecting a co-founder and core team members, friends may not necessarily prove to be best co-founder or core team members. So have an open mind, some people may not be very aligned with the idea and then having an environment of candid feedback should always be there. But some people might still want to keep one foot in some other business or some other job while working with you on your startup. So be aware of the fact that if the commitment level from different founders is different then it is going to be a great balancing act to maintain relationships as well as keep the ball rolling.

(7) As employees or students, we usually become successful with few strengths and with knowledge about only certain aspects of business. As a startup owner, unless there is a solid team from day one, We need to wear several different hats and each aspect is equally

important. If a startup founder is from an engineering background then generally, the intuition is to go and work on technical problems before looking at product-market fit. If the founder is from a marketing background, then there is a tendency to underestimate delays and issues in getting potentially working product and some technical skill required for the product may suddenly become more expensive or less expensive to incorporate in the product. With the great resignation era in 2021 suddenly certain technical solutions became more expensive while with mass layoffs happening in 2022 and recession fear certain technical solutions. So be prepared and keep an eye on macroeconomic conditions in the potential product space.

(8) Work on the product iteratively instead of waiting for this perfect solution with 100 features

incorporated before launch. Market keeps changing and competition is also evolving so it's important to work iteratively with market and keep this wheel churning to eventually reach to most useful solution for the market.

(9) Keep learning from competition and highly successful companies in the same or advancement space check, see the patterns that successful companies are following and try to follow the same as much as possible with your limited resources. Use digital and free marketing as much as possible and be innovative to increase your company and brand awareness. Look for companies that can help to start up your project faster and may provide you with an underlying solution faster instead of trying to invent the wheel again.

For example, if you are trying to launch some app in artificial intelligence space then Live AI dream(www.liveaidream.com) can give you end to end products much faster and with much money. If you are trying to sell some retail product then maybe first using amazon's delivery network by putting it in Amazon stores is much faster and cheaper then establishing your own distribution pipeline end to end. So consider what to outsource and what to do on your own from the beginning.

(10) And if you are not sure what exactly you should build because you have a couple of ideas in mind then instead of getting demotivated check how much money it would take to really launch the idea. Explore if there are any inexpensive ways to create awareness about it and if everything fits in the budget then take an action instead of just thinking about taking action. In this case taking action means launching a demo product or putting up a few example products for sale and trying out the market. However, this all depends on much initial setup and money is required to accomplish and also on the risk appetite of the startup or founder.

(11) Work on mental and physical health proactively, practice meditation, walk, write a journal or whatever works for you to stay focused and filter out noise that brings your energy down.

(12) Have a solid financial plan before starting your own company and also a clear entry and exit criteria so that failures become less daunting and also it helps in staying motivated. As time does not seem too short (don't expect company to take off in one week or one month) be ready for it to take some time but at the same time don't make it unlimited time. in that case you might find it hard to stay disciplined and stay focused to work hard and smart for your startup.

(13) Instead of having a mental plan and ideas, jotting the product ideas and plans on paper really helps. If you have work experience of working in some big corporation before starting your own company then you know each stage that is followed in the particular product segment and follow all the stages one by one even in your own startup. Since all those pitch deck slides, product plan, interface and call flow diagrams etc. will give better clarity and insight to you as well

(14) Learn to celebrate life as you go and start enjoying the journey instead of just walking to reach some destination. Be kind along the way and make relationships along the way as social capital is possibly the most important thing that helps in unexpected ways apart from all the above mentioned things is that are more generic some of the things are applicable to specific industries and those things can make a huge difference in your experience of setting up a startup.

For example, there might be some important meetups or conferences related to your industry that can give huge insight about what is coming up in the near future. Discover what is already launched and what is already successful and probably hard to compete with and what is already launched and failed. We can learn a great deal from all sorts of companies, even companies that could not sustain sharing their stories and write ups and mention about what went in their blind spot or what problems they overlooked.

So, knowing names of both failed and successful companies and doing market research is probably the first and most important step for your startup. Awareness of best tools in the trait and help systems, free education, mentoring circles, resource pool and in general knowing the ecosystem for startup is very important and make the decisions more sound. Also networking with people is sometimes so insightful and fulfilling.

You cannot gain so much information in even much more money and time from books or courses as much as you can get by talking to people. But it's a double edged sword, if what you are looking for is not clear and conversation is not pleasant then might end up getting even more confused and feel demotivated by perceived success of all the other big companies and successful startups that made millions or billions of dollars very early in their journey.

It is important to understand that every company has its own life cycle and as long as you have a clear path in mind and others success should only motivate you and others failure should only educate you but nothing should be able to demotivate you.

Perseverance is probably the important factor in making something that is so worthwhile to have

successful. There will be times when you have to cut back on expenses that you used to never consider as an expense and you have to work continuously nonstop without any results in sight for weeks or months, but if I do what others are not doing right now. Then you can have what others can't have later.

Keep that NorthStar in sight, always know your destination, keep both short term and long milestones and targets in mind and try to achieve those. At the same time, be aware as a startup owner we cannot assume that we have full control on outcome. If we do the perfect execution of the best possible idea still there's a 50% chance of it not working. But remember that in this journey nothing is really a failure as long as you have not spread yourself too thin. Financially and you are enjoying this learning process.

Remember that having your own company should make us more modest, more respectful, more skillful and better networked then when we were students, or we were working as employees. If nothing, it should make you a better person and better employee in the worst case.

Many people share statistics that 90% startups fail but that is a blanket statement it is as true as something similarly pessimistic is. For example, all human beings lie. Yes, all human beings might lie at some point in their life but that does not mean that all beings are liar this statement needs more information.

Similarly, 90% of startups fail. That does not mean that your startup will fail, What preparation

What did the owner do before starting the company? How much money and time was put into it? How motivated was the owner? Did the owner have enough social circle, knowledge of the topic or hiring capacity? Was market analysis done? How much money and effort was invested in sales, from start to beginning? What was the commitment level of founders? There are so many more things that need to be taken into account. And more importantly after the failure of the startup did the founder re-bounced with an even better and more successful startup or career or not.

So, once we take into account all this we know that we are not doing something that is achievable, it is just the road less traveled may be the road to Hannah (you know what I am saying if you have been to Hawaii).

Some experiences are worth trying if you have the personality and passion for it, it

can be a long , windy, uncomfortable, yet adventurous road. Though costly and may be a risky journey but with proper planning and if you are the correct match in terms of attitude and what you want in life then it is an unparalleled experience. You must try it but with a proper plan start early, keep a buffer in mind both in terms of resources, money, changing demands from factors that are outside your control and after you are sure you know enough driving to navigate such routes while enjoying the journey.

On a specific journey, the things that really helped me are using social media platforms like Facebook and LinkedIn to share more information about the product and get feedback early. Also, on LinkedIn since my past work helped me to establish my technical brand and credibility, so it became easier to find collaborators, partners, employees, and investors early on in my journey. Also going to startup expos and meet up events in person help me to listen to other startup owner's stories, experiences, make some new connections and potential collaborators.

Also, I got to listen to many different marketing, sales and other startup founders' pitches so it gave me insights into what to think early on in my journey. While enjoying connecting with people, having high energy events with so many passionate people in the same space, such events give a very unique perspective about how things are really working in different segments.

How big corporations think very differently than startups. What are the innovative ideas to

increase product reachability, how to seek investment, when to invest, how to negotiate terms, how to create solid documentation etc.

Learn from as many people and as many sources as possible but also be aware of the fact that people who have their first experience of starting their own company generally have less and very structured feedback to give. The people that have never started their own company and just thought about it have much more feedback to give.

Many people will tell you along the way how special you are as a founder and how successful your company can be. Also, many people will also tell along the way how crazy it is to try to set up your own startup and how every idea that you think is brilliant is already launched or has no customer base for it. Some will be more balanced and will say it sounds like a good idea but before doing anything do market analysis and in some cases, people will come back to your product market analysis to tell you how it can or cannot be successful.

The only thing that I would say is your journey is only your journey. Listen to every feedback carefully and see what you can use from it for course correction. Don't forget to show your gratitude to people who have spent their precious moments of life guiding you. But the feedback should have an impact on your motivation level. As an employee we get so much feedback on our tasks, but we don't stop doing them. We think about the review comments and incorporate it without attaching ourselves too much with the outcome or without involving our prestige with it. More importantly without getting demotivated from it. It is exactly the same thing as a business owner. Whenever you are getting feedback you should just take the feedback for what it is, it is to see if your plan is foolproof or not and whether you think there is any other better way to do it or not. And if you are confident then just go ahead with it.

But it is easier said than done and at such times when we feel low, when we feel demotivated and when We feel that we have made a big mistake. It is crucial to have a support system. Make sure you have a few cheerleaders in your life who make you feel good and make sure no matter what is going with your startup you have no right to be rude or ignorant with people around you. Clearly communicate your work hours, your availability and passion for the work but make sure to be respectable, show the important small gestures of care and keep your close circle even closer. If you have no emotional support system then things become much more difficult than imagined.

Make sure to thank people whose work or educational videos or guidance you're leveraging. Make sure to give due credit to people and keep your effort for business separate from your persona. What we do as startup founders is for our selfish reasons, for our own vision and with our long-term goals in mind. So, our family and close circle should not pay for it. They are already extra accommodating for us by providing that mental blanket of warmth in this cold journey that doesn't make them pay more by letting them know how frustrated, lonely and rejected you might feel at certain times.

Since all these things are like a badge of honors. If we look at any documentary of mountain climbers. For example, people who went on Himalaya expeditions always show the bruises, wounds and frost bite toes for the climbers in those documentaries because all those things make documentaries worth watching. In the case of setting up our own startup we are making a documentary of our life. We are the story writers, we are the climbers, and we are the directors of this story but our crew is what is making it feasible. What is going to make it successful is that without a proper support crew it is much harder to make the same documentary in the same amount of time and money.

So, while it is important to dedicate ourselves to our craft and our new startup, it is also important to realize that it is just a part of life and the entire environment around it is the most important ingredient in it. With constant effort even a small rope can leave a mark on stone but for the rope to be able to do that it is important that it does it so silently and so persistently without making any irritating or uncomfortable screeching sounds.

In my case I am extremely blessed to have a very supportive family who keeps me grounded, who are not just giving me mental strength but sometimes even provide funding for my business or help me navigate certain situations. And even my coworkers from previous companies are extremely helpful and they keep calling me asking me how they can help. The world is almost like a mirror in many cases the day when I wake up and think it is a good day and i will do these two things today by the time the day ends. I usually find answers in some random YouTube video or while walking in the park and talking to some neighbor or something very usual.

We get what we look for. So, it is important to be less confused and more confident and have faith that things will work out to really make things work out. Similarly, it is important to know that this journey is long, full of ups and downs but very few fortunate people get to live their dream and ever fewer have somebody to support them with comforting words so one thing we should make sure we don't lose in this journey is those people that support us in every situation and our own health. It is quite possible that we just keep sitting in one place with our laptop for days and weeks.

Initially and completely get poured into this passion, at least that's what I did. But it's a big mistake any player who has ever been successful in their game has always kept themselves mentally and physically fit even while getting no tangible results for great effort. But they still kept doing it and improving at it and adding more and more sharpness, more awareness of their competitor tactics and kept growing at their skill to eventually be able to make it to the finish line. This is exactly what a startup owner has to do for a few weeks and months. Maybe there is no tangible result but that does not mean that your startup has failed. You just need to keep reviving your strategy and product for your company.

In this day and age of social media there is a false sense of success and happiness everywhere. People are always mentioning how somebody got big funding, somebody got very successful product and how things were just so smooth for some owners with investors lined up from day one. Read those stories for what they are, just the stories and don't feel affected by it. At max note down the company and investor search for the owner interviews and investor portfolio and see if there are any takeaways from it.

One thing that is really important in my journey and this is also part of my goal is to emerge as a better and more skilled person at the other end. A leader that employees can look up to who is caring who has watched out for them from day one. A partner who fulfills its promises and communicates the risks upfront and most importantly a deserving leader of a very successful artificial intelligence company. But all these goals also mean that I need to read about many different types of topics each day, wear different hats and work on different problems, as a startup founder especially early on we are everything we are the IT person, sales head, marketing, customer care, technician, and engineer so it is important to plan day in advance keep it bucketed for different work items.

And I can't stress enough to meditate whenever possible to keep your mind sharp and focused. It gives access to a more relaxed, focused and stress free mind that is very active and free to absorb new things like a sponge. In all these details, one thing that I have mentioned only slightly about is finance. There are many people who will try to set up a startup along with their full-time job and such people share many examples of similar success stories.

There are many people who are working both as consultants or in part time jobs for a company for a few days a week and side by side setting up a startup and some people setting up a startup with no other parallel track. I am in the third category. I dedicated myself one percent to startup setup. While not having monthly income was always a bothersome thought after earning as a salaried employee for so long, I can't imagine doing it any other way since so much energy, time and effort is required for the process.

However, everybody have different situation and that's why every individual have a different

problem to solve. But if it is possible to financially plan ahead for complete dedicated effort for business then focus improves a lot. Also, there are so many ways nowadays to get funding, but in my case, I realized that taking funding is not as easy as it sounds. It also takes considerable energy and time early on to find investors and also implications of it can be significant so from a social status perspective it sounds very flashy that a startup has already secured some funding, and somebody is putting their money behind it. But after digging some more I felt it is worth it to take business from idea to product stage without involving investors.

It allows you to change the story and shift your business from one to another very easily when you are still exploring what exactly your company should be doing. And you will be able to hold much more of a share of the company if it is already a product. The product does two things for the company, one it communicates that the founding team has capability to make the product and the idea is feasible. Second investors can easily see that you are invested and committed to the idea, so they feel more comfortable in taking the risk on your company.

There are many startup competitions for initial seed funding money, many other funding strategies like crowdfunding, investing your own money, taking loan, taking funding from the government if your company is in a certain sector and meets certain criteria. This was one thing that I spent my time very early on and got aware of what are the requirements to get funding. Some documentation is common that we should do for any of these options and some things helped in strategizing action plans.

But navigating all this space was very difficult, especially the fear of unknown what if I end up signing some contract that I should not know what terms and clauses should be there, and other such questions were very difficult to answer since most of the people around me did not have experience in raising funds. In that case, taking guidance from a mentor turned out really useful for me. There are many mentor groups that provide free or paid mentorship. I went for free mentorship and my mentor himself being a successful venture capitalist saved a lot of time in navigating the path early on.

As a founder since I felt I don't want to get funding in idea stage of company so i was very reluctant to put pitch deck in place but since my mentor suggested to do it. So, I went ahead with and put together a pitch deck that entire exercise turned out to be so useful that I could quickly put together my website and first demo version for the product since while putting together the pitch deck I had to think about details in a structured way and it helped me with detailed planning for the product and change certain aspects about it to capture growth opportunity.

In parallel with pitch decks another important thing is registering a company very early on and registering it with the correct type.

It requires quite a bit of knowledge about state taxes, different legal terms, where to register, how to register and similar information. After the entire process I felt so good since I got to learn and explore so many different aspects of business and I had new found respect for businesses that are operating in more than one country.

Also, if you are considering registering a company in more than one country then it has so many other considerations involved. I was able to take guidance from the owner of a multimillion company to navigate the path correctly and select the right options and conditions while registering with the company. So, making sure that there is always a mentor or guide by your side who have done it previously saves so many costly mistakes for the company. For the hosting company website also, I considered many different options but then ended up creating and hosting it in-house with my friends' help and saved a lot of money and effort with experienced people guiding me along the way.

As a startup owner, one very important aspect of life I realized is, there are so many people who are ready to help and so many people who are watching and drawing inspiration from our journey and really want us to be successful that it is just a matter of asking help and then you would get at least one expert who is willing to help. But the energy flows both ways make sure people feel appreciated and respected for what they are doing for you since whoever is spending time for your startup is making a choice of not doing something else in that time and doing a favor by being there for you so make sure to remember it always and pay it back and pay it forward whenever possible.

In fact, I spoke to a few investors, who approached me through social media. I clearly told them that I was not looking for investment in the idea stage but what kind guidance they can give me to avoid mistakes and I was pleasantly surprised how insightful those discussions were and how much time it saved me. Similar story I have for marketing and advertising as well. So, the gist of sharing all these details is that as a founder we need to acknowledge that there are experts in every area and we as one person or as one team have only limited knowledge.

Saying that we are exploring this area and we welcome their feedback opens so many doors for us and early feedback is as precious as somebody investing money without asking for shares in the company. But after taking care of all the surrounding aspects the main question was still looking me in the face, what about the product. It needs so many different types of skills and so much technical expertise to build it that too without external investment. Well, the answer was by not getting overwhelmed and by trusting technical competence of my team and hiring freelancers wherever absolutely needed.

For growing from niche set of skills to many different type of skills I had to learn to learn one thing that I adopted was to listen to videos at 2x speed since the artificial intelligence space is growing so fast that it is very important to stay updated so knowledge about latest tools meant something that can be directly leveraged just by the knowledge latest updates in the industry. I also designed and created an automated system to quickly take my idea into a well tested product. And as fate would have it, instead of the original idea becoming successful, this automation toolkit became more successful. I was able to get many companies and early startups approaching me for the product. And once the ball starts rolling then effort required reduces or I should say we get adapted to the process and become mentally much more resilient and prepared to scale the business.

And last but not the least hiring employees that have good communication skills, and who align with your company values and vision is not easy since you can't pay top dollars early on in the journey, but it is extremely crucial so select your core team and employees very carefully and be very clear from the beginning how are you going to compensate your team for their hard work and loyalty. Again financial planning and setting clear charter your company is very important what will be financial model revenue, per user cost, monthly projected target etc., employee's salary, employee bonus, founding members compensation and how much to invest back in the business along with many other such financial factors.

Without clear financial planning it is almost impossible to recruit or retain capable and committed

employees. And any company is only as good as its employees. So, taking care of recruitment in the right way and getting involved in the well-being of employees is the most important task of

any leader and if you are founder and chief executing officer then dedicate some time in your calendar for ensuring that the health of the company in terms of policies, employees happiness, growth opportunities and compensation is always in place and well defined.

There are so many things that as startup founders we learn each day and we get to talk to so many other CEOs, venture capitalists, founders and experienced marketing and sales executives. This journey is all about getting 1% better each day at something. And then translate it into value for your end customer and for your employees.

Many people keep calling me and asking me what triggered this switch. How did I know that I am ready to start my own company? If any of you have this question as well then here is my answer, since I always had this long term vision in my mind. I had a list of things to learn and a list of skills to develop along with a financial plan where I can sustain without any income for a set period of time so soon as

Those boxes checked and I switched to the other side without wasting a single day.

Making that hard switch had its cost but I knew if I am not disciplined about my journey then this journey either would never start and or it will never reach any significant destination. Even till today, I have a very specific plan for the day each day and till the plan is executed I don't stop. Being a startup owner means being disciplined and focused.

Another question that I get asked a lot is did I start alone or did I have a team from the beginning. Well, as crazy as it sounds, I started alone. And then explored and figured out who to partner with. In this entire journey my husband has been my strength, he is playing so many roles for this journey to be successful and I feel that I have married my biggest fan. Even when I am not sure if I am doing the right thing, can I be successful? He always knows I will be successful. Early on I was thinking of taking up some side consultant job for 2 days a week or some way to generate monthly income but he kept telling me to have faith in my ability and no way i could fail. I can either be successful or highly successful.

He took care of many financial and family related responsibilities that earlier I used to manage and always asked me why am I not outsourcing certain tasks and why am I trying to avoid investing more in the business? He was the first investor in my business who is completely aligned with my business proposition and has full faith in my ability and my company values. For any woman entrepreneur I guess having a partner, who can be the pillar of strength in this journey, is just so important.

This is one thing that has an impact on every moment of your journey. Having peace at home while so many things are in churn in your professional life is just extremely important. I am not a married woman but also a mother so the next thing that i was afraid about in the beginning was. What would it mean for my child, would I have enough time to give to them, how will this impact the entire equation. But to my surprise, actually I was less stressed and happier while doing all the work for my company. I could give more focused time and attention to my child and her performance also improved in various aspects.

No wonder that we had to cut back on our lavish trips and mindless shopping sessions since now we were changing the financial aspects of our life. But my daughter appreciated the fact that I was working so hard and I looked much more content and happier while doing that. She in fact, started putting her study table beside my work desk and started being even more focused, even more in whatever she was doing. She even asked me if focused and challenging work makes the skin shine. I did not know the answer, but I know that if we really want to do something and if we are hundred percent prepared to face any situation in the journey then there is really no way to stop somebody. It is possible that the first product idea would fail, but then keep doing course correction and try the improved idea or just try a different idea and something will work eventually.

I have a theory that if we really want to cook tasty food we need to be in a happy state of mind. If music puts one in a happy state of mind then put some music on and then start cooking. Somehow it always tastes better when we cook it when we are in a happy state of mind. And the same thing applies to everything else as well. If we meet someone and we have high positive energy then the other person starts smiling automatically with us and the entire conversation becomes very pleasant, and people tend to remember the conversation and the person for much longer than otherwise. Having a cheerful outlook and ignoring or stopping the things that are draining our energy is another important thing that helped me a lot.

When we make such a transition many relationships around us also change some for good and some for not so good. Expecting those changes and just avoiding reacting and shielding yourself from changes in the environment, need a lot of mental strength but it is an important skill to learn as an entrepreneur. When we have the control of our happiness within us and motivation within us then rewards from the external world especially materialistic rewards affect little less. And we learn to work without any expectations for a very long time. However, working without expectations does not mean working on anything and everything, we need to stay focused on the plan we created in the beginning and stay the course with it. And slowly we start to see people and recognize people whose faces light up every time they see us irrespective of how much money we are making and how useful we can be now for them, to other types of people. And being able to make that distinction is what we call experience.

My mother has always been my inspiration since the beginning of my life and she knows nothing about what artificial intelligence is and what it can do. And initially she tried to warn me to not leave a stable job. But once she realized that I am much happier and so quickly making progress in my startup's journey she became my second investor and biggest advisor. It is so funny that we feel a certain way about our parents and we feel they won't know certain things if they never tried it. But at least in my case, I don't have to communicate how I feel to my mother and she understands from the tone of my voice.

And to my surprise my mother started following up news about artificial intelligence and started giving me leads about opportunities in certain areas and even suggested me to attend certain

conferences that I didn't realize were happening. It is just a matter of having faith and starting your journey and people who genuinely love us come along anyway. The same goes with my father. He helped me register a company in another country, followed up different laws and different nuances in the process and contributed every time by saying don't worry about money, just go ahead and live your dream.

I guess that is why I named my company "Live AI Dream". I want to live my dream and to help other people also with their dreams by democratizing artificial intelligence so that even small and medium business owners can also easily incorporate it. Kindness always comes in a circle once we give kindness we receive kindness and the circle goes on. Sometimes there might be a delay but don't let the circle break from your side. My brother has always been my role model in terms of how analytical, sorted, balanced and a great leader he is. And every day after coming from work he spoke to me for hours to resolve all my queries and doubts about technical and non-technical things.

Sometimes he even sat down and figured out the cost of executing option A versus option B. Which would have taken me days to figure out. Having support from family is just invaluable and if you have it, consider yourself lucky and in this up down journey keep track of your emotions, words and expressions and don't end up losing more important things. Many people say" having a startup is risky" (especially if you are leaving a very well paying job), they say it from a financial perspective but your company will always compensate for that money if it becomes successful.

And if not then the invaluable experience that you would gain during this journey that will help you secure a better job later. But the risk really is your mental health and watching for self-expression, if the company does well, don't boast about it and if it does not do well don't stay frustrated, that is mostly what it is all about.

Even the mentors that we have in our professional and academic journey so far, play a significant role in the entire process. So, make sure to stay connected with your leads, mentors and professors. They have achieved lot of respect and success in their career already and they become more like well-wishers and guide for us who just want to see us successful. They notice such small things about our communication style, our leadership style, our execution style and they can really share insight on what we should outsource to somebody else and how we should handle ourselves.

And this is an especially important perspective to take into account early on. And these mentors also know a lot about industry and how the corporate world functions and how 'things around here work'. If we are pitching some product proposition to another company's CEO versus to a project manager. That pitch needs to be different in a very subtle way and we need to cover and highlight distinct aspects of the product when pitching to different stakeholders. Since we want to connect to what they are looking for, what vocabulary is most important to include in the deck, these insights our mentors know much better than we do and these things make a difference between a product that made no sales versus a successful product.

The startup journey is all about constantly learning, constantly getting rejected, constantly adapting and improving. After one product gets some traction and we get some customers, we should not assume that the journey becomes easier from here, because it is far from the truth. Scaling business with time is also a particularly challenging aspect since the founder's involvement with each and every task has to be reduced slowly and we need to have a capable and motivated team that can take ownership of tasks and make our vision a reality.

Not getting carried away in the process and considering projected sales only as a projection is another important aspect to avoid hiring too quickly. Diverse types of pricing models for the company's offerings also play a very important role in the long term financial well-being of the company. And always keeping a buffer in our promises to customers and to employees is important. If our technical team thinks that the product will be ready on x date, then that is not the date we can commit to the customer. We have to keep a buffer for delays.

Similarly, if projected sales are motivating to hire at a fast pace, then we should make sure the data is really correct. We are not ignoring macroeconomic conditions and we have enough buffer for financial setbacks as well as some other products that the same workforce can contribute to if one product does not take off and other similar strategies.

I have covered my journey as a founder so far, but I haven't narrowed down on why I was motivated to solve this particular problem that I have setup my business around. And what made me so passionate about it, what kind of value it can bring and why am I qualified to solve it. Maybe some insight on this aspect of my journey would help you to narrow down your specific motivation as well.

I think artificial intelligence (AI) is going to be the most disruptive technology of this century and it would really matter who are the participants when this technology is still getting defined and it is still an active topic of research. Through this technology every sector will get impacted including healthcare, education, security, travel, construction, entertainment, communication, and everything. So, there is a need that everybody should have a say in it and this technology is deployed in an inclusive, efficient, and responsible manner. Right now, there are very few women engineers and women leaders working on this technology and as a result there are some use cases and some data points that are getting completely missed by this technology.

And even all the research and adoption of the technology is by very large corporations , these corporations have become very efficient at certain tasks while small and medium businesses don't know how to start incorporating AI in their business model since there is a huge initial investment cost and for deploying this technology in production needs very specific type of experience and skill set that only large companies are able to afford for now.

To make sure that these two issues get addressed and to showcase to women engineers that it is feasible to contribute to this fast-evolving industry not just as an employee but as a founder of the company as well and to carve a path that can be followed by many future women startups in this domain. I wanted to not just set up my company but also, I wanted to share my story and learning along the way so that they can incorporate some lessons from my journey and avoid some mistakes and pick some best practices along the way.

Another issue that I wanted to solve is to reduce the entry barrier for small businesses and medium size companies with AI usage, so I have developed an end to end pipeline where anyone without any knowledge of AI can incorporate AI in their product with just a few clicks by using our end-to-end pipeline. Also, since we are making AI inclusiveness as our primary goal, we are also educating university students for free and small company owners for free about AI use cases and how it can solve the specific problem in their industry. And since the education is free and through live sessions we are hoping to have significant reach and impact.

The companies that make significant contributions to society have more chances of being successful. Since the purpose of setting up a startup is to quickly make money, then that probably is not strong enough motivation to live through all the ups and downs. But when motivation is to leave a positive impact on the society then the entire ecosystem works in alignment and chances of success are manifold. So

I am taking this path for my selfish reason since I want my company to be respected and remembered for a long time for all the good reasons.

Also, I did my formal education in this area, and worked in this field for several years in a top-notch team of a very renowned company. And I have mentored several startup owners in the AI domain as part of my additional job responsibility (for the venture branch of my previous company) so I am equipped to solve and recognize problems along the way.

Working as a founder of a startup is a delicate balancing act and at every step the growth and learning is just so fulfilling. I love being the CEO and founder of Live AI Dream and this journey is really a dream come true for me. Thank you for patiently reading about my experiences and I hope it could add value for you!

Website: www.liveaidream.com[1]

---

1. http://www.liveaidream.com/

Chapter V: Tangie Holifield: My Journey

Struggle teaches you a lot of things, and I am happy that I witnessed a roller coaster ride. The journey has improved me as a person and made me more mature. - Manoj Bajpayee[1]

Background:

How I define myself: I am a human being, who just happens to be a woman, as a scientist, as a small business owner, a true foodie and an author. These descriptions showcase the multi-dimensions of who I am as a person, as I set goals to pursue my lifelong passions.

---

1. *https://www.brainyquote.com/authors/manoj-bajpayee-quotes*

Being a Southerner, by birth, the things that really matter in life are: family, friends, food and football. And with that being said, I made my debut into the world at a tailgating party during a college football game in Huntsville, Alabama. But that is another story for another time.

Anyone who knows me knows that I love to cook and I am always asked the inevitable questions of: "Who taught you how to cook?" and "Where does your passion for all things edible come from?" For the most part, my circle of family and friends call me a "mad" scientist because of my wicked culinary skills in applying STEM in the kitchen laboratory, where I believe that cooking is both a science and an art. And learning the basics as to how to cook and to continue to cook and reinterpret foods and how we eat in this modern world is a life-long process and a passion, which makes for happy memories, for sure.

Growing up in a military family, I spent most of my childhood between the United States and Germany, where my family and I took the opportunity to travel extensively throughout Europe. It was during those summer vacations, returning stateside, to the warmth and bustle of my grandmother's kitchen farmhouse, which became my training ground for learning to cook traditional Southern dishes.

My grandmother, who was professionally trained and who served several Alabama governors, a senator, and later, the most elite families along the River Bluffs Community along the Tennessee River in Florence, Alabama, and after all these years, I can remember like it was yesterday, when it all started for me at the age of three in my Gran's kitchen. There was nothing more satisfying than being in the kitchen with my beloved Grand who put me on a very tall stool, because I could not reach the counter, as she allowed me to crack the eggs we just gathered from the hen house to bake a cake.

And the greatest reward that day was being able to lick the mixing bowl clean. And then through my adolescent years it was the assortment of aunts and uncles who would share their talents for cooking with me as well. And like many of the family recipes, nothing was ever written down; it was a matter of oral history being passed from one generation to another.

As for most of my academic life and career in the real world, I have been a research soil scientist for over 28 years. My career in soils and the environmental sciences was actually inspired by my grandfather, who was a farmer, a blacksmith and a laborer who helped build the Wilson Dam, which began construction in 1918 and completed in 1924, spanning the Tennessee River between Lauderdale County and Colbert County in Alabama. He cultivated his own special hybrid blackberries and made dandelion wine, as well as being an avid huntsman and loved fishing in the Tennessee River.

But becoming a soil scientist almost did not happen. While attending graduate school in upstate New York, I seriously considered quitting my doctoral studies to pursue a culinary education at the Culinary Institute of America in Hyde Park, New York, but that dream of being a chef was deferred and I settled into a career of being a research soil scientist. And all the while, I was honing my skills as a serious foodie and home cook.

Since then, I have added my own signature style and adapted the recipes to make them simple and accessible. My scientific training has lent an air of precision to my cooking as I experiment with melding classic preparations with new and exciting flavors.

And now, in spending more than two decades working as a research soil scientist and educator, my experiences have led to me being an advocate for sustainable practices—when gathering food from the land or the sea. Something else I learned from both my grandparents who had a farm and lived off the land. Not being one to brag, I am also the co-author of a guide to urban farming distributed by the USDA and I actively promote sustainable food choices through the recipe selections on my blog, On the Menu @ Tangie's Kitchen.

Often cooking with the vegetables that I grow in my own backyard, I am inspired by the Southern foods cooked by my grandmother and the global cuisines of Africa, Europe, South America, and Asia. I truly find inspiration in traveling, visiting the farmers market, seeking out street food vendors, and reminiscing with friends and family about the meals they have enjoyed over the years.

My passion for global travel seems to go hand- in- hand with my hobby of photography and my obsession with all things edible. My adventures have led to collecting authentic recipes that I have adapted to the traditional Southern dishes I learned first-hand from grandmother. My experiences in my grandmother's kitchen laid the foundation for me in creating my own original recipes with the flavors of the South, like "Catfish Vindaloo", where Northern India meets the Deep South.

My unique experiences have taught me that food is the one universal element that is common to all of humanity, regardless of international boundaries or cultural heritage and differences. Food is also the common bond in all things that connects us with Nature, with our families, with our friends and the memories across a lifetime. I have spent most of my life in academia and research, but the one common thread to the many aspects of my life was food, particularly how to grow it, how to prepare it and how to share the fruits of my labors with others.

Cooking was my sanctuary from the rigors of the workplace. And the kitchen has been my refuge where I could commune with the spirits of my ancestors, but most importantly, I could connect with the spirit of my Grand. For me cooking is about love and down South when a dish was cooked exceptionally well and enjoyed by all, it was said that "She put her foot in it!" And if your mind "ain't right" when you enter the kitchen, you can forget about preparing a well cooked meal, for it only spell disaster when your heart is not in your cooking. And it shows visually on the plate, as well as the unappealing lack of flavor to the palette.

My unique experiences have taught me that sharing food is the one universal element common to all of humanity, regardless of international boundaries or cultural heritage and differences.

Industry:

Given my background, one can see that my passion for travel and my deep Southern roots laid the foundation for my lifetime love of cooking. These experiences eventually led me to the industry I most identify with, the food service industry, where my businesses have focused on catering operations, and the manufacturing of consumer individual-sized packaged products designed for retail sale.

My first business venture into the food service industry as an entrepreneur began with a lemonade stand at the age of 9 years old. During that summer, I managed to earn nearly $10,000.00 by using the resources available to me and by utilizing successful marketing strategies. What I learned from that summer in selling lemonade were four crucial strategies I still use today:

Learn to be fearless and be willing to take a risk.

As a business person, you cannot sit quietly behind the counter, waiting patiently for customers to arrive. You have to be fearless. It does not matter if you are selling lemonade as a kid or a sales representative for a fortune 500 company, you have to be outgoing, passionate, fearless and willing to take risks to succeed. Too often, entrepreneurs take an academic view of product sales. I find it that it is so easy to fall into the trap of the "if you build it they will come" mentality. From my experience, the only way to sell any product is the old fashion way: to hit the pavement, knock on doors, and put yourself out there in a very raw and vulnerable way.

Build your brand.

I employed several other girls from the neighborhood. Our specialty was pink lemonade. Given that I had three stands at three different locations, all the stands had to look the same for brand identity. As a kid, I saw how McDonald's was able to incorporate itself as a brand, so took notice and used that as a model. So I had pink t-shirts made and required all the employees to wear pink satin ribbons in their hair. And it worked!

Do your research and know your market(s).

My three lemonade stands locations were set up throughout the neighborhood: one at the bank, one at the grocery store, and one at the post office. The stands would be set up every two weeks, timed with the arrival of the bi-weekly paycheck. Most of my customers were military personnel and civilian employees.

Always be cross-selling.

Lemonade was not the only product being sold at the stand. Cookies, Chips and Brownies were always on hand to sell to willing and regular customers. As kids, we would be shouting "Lemonade! Cookies! Come and get 'em" at the top of our lungs. Sure enough, people started coming over to our lemonade stands to see the source of the commotion. In a matter of minutes, we had a line of customers queued up and ready to help serve them while utilizing this "unique" form of advertising.

And yes, at the end of day, a healthy profit can be made by selling lemonade and those earnings enabled me to start my own college fund.

Another source of inspiration for developing the entrepreneur mindset also came from my grandmother. She also ran a small catering business, in addition to holding a full time job, raising a family, and managing a farm. It was also during my summer vacations that she made sure that I stayed busy assisting her in baking cakes and pies for one function or another happening in the community. What I learned from my grandmother is that you really have to love what you are doing, and hopefully, the gift you have brought to the table is making a difference in someone's life, even if it is as simple as preparing a meal or baking a cake.

Another pivotal work experience occurred at the age of 15, when I was employed by the Department of Defense as a clerk typist with typing and business skills that I had honed in the 6th grade. Through this work experience, I learned time management, crucial communication skills in drafting business letters and how to resolve issues through reliable and effective customer service.

Whether one recognizes or not every step that you take in your life prepares you for the next level in the journey that you are taking to achieve those goals you have set for yourself......but I digress.

While holding down a full time job, as a research soil scientist, my early childhood experiences eventually led me to start my own business, "The Lunch Box", a Catering and Food Delivery service specializing in cold and hot lunches for one, in 2013. Subsequently, the profits from "The Lunch Box" venture lead to the launching of my next business venture, "Miss Jenny's Jellies & Jams™ in 2014, an online specialty gourmet shop, named in honor of my grandmother. This business features handcrafted products using fresh seasonal produce and all natural ingredients. We produce small batches using traditional water canning methods without preservatives to ensure the best flavor and the highest quality products for the enjoyment of foodies like me, everywhere in the world. In the future, I plan to expand these products to include salsas, sauces, marmalades, fruit spreads, preserves, conserves, chutneys, pickles, and pickled vegetables and fruits.

Inspiration for many of my business adventures organically grows from one idea to the next, constantly evolving. But I always have a business plan in place to help me navigate each business venture that I undertake, allowing me to utilize my unique skill set. This led me to creating a food blog and eventually led to me writing a cookbook.

And speaking of the cookbook, I was basically inspired by family members and friends who were constantly asking me for the recipes of the dishes that I had prepared and later posting the finished dish on my personal facebook page and my blog, to write a cookbook. My love for cooking has always been a big part of my life, mainly because I find it so soothing to be in a kitchen preparing a meal with the freshest, locally sourced ingredients that I can find.

As a home cook, it's easy to get stuck in a recipe rut. Just grabbing a cookbook from the shelf and watching as it falls open to those handful of well-worn pages can do little to inspire one to cook. More often than not, that's where our decision-making stops, and we find ourselves gravitating to these same meals time after time.

Writing the cookbook was a fairly easy process. However, the real challenge that presented itself to me was writing a well crafted book proposal. What I also discovered is that it is so difficult to find a publisher that is truly interested in publishing an unknown and untried author, especially in a market that is saturated with so many home cooks and celebrity chefs. After numerous rejections of my book proposal, I decided to take the self publishing route, using the modest profits from Miss Jenny's Jellies and jams to publish, "On The Menu@ Tangie's Kitchen: The Celebration of Spring".

"The Celebration of Spring" is dedicated to the way we are eating right now, and features recipes for traditional and innovative dishes based on regional cooking found in the Southern United States and influenced by the global cuisines of Africa, Asia, Europe and South America.

Written with easy-to-follow instructions, the range of recipes in The Celebration of Spring focuses on sustainable ingredients that can be found at almost any local grocery store or farmers market. Full-color photographs that are delightful to look at along with helpful tips and charts that are also included to bring the full cooking experience to you at your fingertips. I hope that this book will inspire confidence in the home cook by offering up a range of new flavors and possibilities to explore and experience at the dinner table.

Highlights of Success:

Personally, I don't think I have lived long enough to have great highlights or a real success story to share.......at this time.

But seriously, how do I define success in life? As I have reviewed Webster Collegiate Dictionary to remind me, the definition of success, which is the opposite of failure, is also defined as "the status of an individual having achieved and accomplished an aim, objective, a desired vision and/or planned goals. Furthermore, success can be a certain social status that describes a prosperous person that could also have gained fame for its favorable outcome." Webster's dictionary continues to define success as the following: "the attaining of wealth, prosperity and/or fame".

I think that the ultimate definition of success, depends on the individual and every person is thinking differently about being prosperous in life and is defining success in their own way, so there cannot exist a one-size fits all definition that is suitable for every human being. It is very important that each individual knows exactly how to define success in THEIR life! Make yourself aware what accomplishment, success, and prosperity in general means to you in your life. Some might define success as having luxurious cars and a huge mansion, whereas others consider a life full of joy and happiness with their family as the true meaning of success. Once you have figured out what is important for you personally, I truly believe that you are able to focus on your visions and goals. And that is what I have done throughout my life, so far.

For me, one of the most important steps to achieving success in life is knowing that I have meaning and purpose to account for the successes in my personal life. If you are not happy with what you are doing in life, then success is as elusive as scarlet pimpernel in winter. The true meaning of success for me goes way beyond the common modern definitions of success, such as having a lot of money, being wealthy, having a lot of tangible and material things, education and a number of earned academic degrees. In my opinion, success in life cannot be measured with the above-named factors, but instead with the amount of people that I am able to help in making a better life for themselves.

I think the highlights of my success are better left to my obituary because that will be the true account of how I have lived my life and what I have created in making this world a better place for everyone. The best advice that I can give to any one is that you never stop doing what you love, because along the way, whether you know it or not, someone is watching and someone will be inspired.

Your ideas and agenda for "What's Next":

In terms of "What's Next" on both a professional level, a business level and personal and spiritual levels, I plan to set new goals with a different set of deliverables or accomplishments. Professionally, at this stage in my life, I am still currently employed full-time, but retirement may be on the horizon sooner than I think. So there is a five year plan in place to reach a certain financial goal, so that I can function comfortably in "retirement" while I pursue my next set of goals for my business ventures.

In terms of looking at my short term goals for what is next on the business agenda is that I am looking to expand the retail market for "Miss Jenny's Jellies & Jams" beyond the on-line store concept. It is time to review the original business plan and make adjustments as needed. Another short term goal is that I will continue to write a series of seasonal cookbooks, over the course of the next five years. I am constantly cooking and developing my own recipes and maintaining my food blog and other social media sites that help keep things on track.

As for a mid-term goal, I want to develop a series of cooking and demonstration workshops that can be presented in various cities, targeting the home cook. I believe that these presentations will help to demystify the processes and techniques in preparing a well-crafted home meal that can be enjoyed by family and friends gathered at the table. I am in the process of developing a business plan and securing the resources to help facilitate this goal.

Perhaps the most ambitious long term goal that I have set for myself is my desire to reach a national audience via appearances on programs such as "Good Morning America" and "The Today Show." And to develop my cooking and lifestyle television show for public television or for a cable network. On a personal and spiritual level, my goals are set for the continuation of my business ventures and I continue to utilize my creativity to have a positive impact on others.

And I believe this can be achieved by continuing to grow and expand by business ventures by creating economic opportunities to improve the community in which I live in and to participate in outreach projects for young people and in being a mentor for those that aspire to contribute to society in a meaningful way.

It's not easy to juggle the many facets of my life, and one must find the balance and understand that it takes time to accomplish those goals that have been set. I also realize that in order for me to reach my goals, I have to surround myself with like minded people who can mentor, support and nurture my ideas and in the process, build a team to make sure that these ideas become goals and these goals become accomplishments, which ultimately leads to success.

Website: https://www.tangieholifield.com/
Facebook: @therealtangieholifield
Instagram: @tangieholifield
Twitter: @tangieholifield
Pinterest: @tangieholifield/on-the-menu-tangies-kitchen

Don't miss out!

Visit the website below and you can sign up to receive emails whenever Au'loni Media Group, LLC publishes a new book. There's no charge and no obligation.

https://books2read.com/r/B-A-TMVR-FGBEC

BOOKS2READ

Connecting independent readers to independent writers.

About the Author

Au'loni Media Group, LLC was most recently selected as the 2022 Philadelphia Awards in the areas of Business and Coaching! We focus on merging traditional media with modern technology. Through Broadcast, Digital, and Print Media, we minimize the gatekeeper's influence over the voice of the underrepresented and disenfranchised, to better strengthen our global community.

Read more at www.amgroupllc.biz/melanoidchronicles.